# BEGINNING BAROQUE FOR PIANO

**Boston Music Company**

*part of The Music Sales Group*

London / New York / Paris / Sydney / Copenhagen / Berlin / Madrid / Tokyo

Published by
**Boston Music Company**
14-15 Berners Street, London W1T 3LJ, UK.

Exclusive Distributors:
**Music Sales Limited**
Distribution Centre, Newmarket Road,
Bury St Edmunds, Suffolk IP33 3YB, UK.
**Music Sales Corporation**
257 Park Avenue South, New York, NY10010, USA.
**Music Sales Pty Limited**
120 Rothschild Avenue,
Rosebery, NSW 2018, Australia.

Order No. BM12320
ISBN 0-184609-815-7

This book © Copyright 2006
**Boston Music Company**
a division of Music Sales Limited.

Series Editor David Harrison.
Music edited by Rachel Payne.
Cover designed by Michael Bell Design.
Cover images: Vivaldi courtesy of Roger Viollet Collection,
Bach and Handel courtesy of Hulton Archive/Getty.
Printed in the EU.

Your Guarantee of Quality
As publishers, we strive to produce every book to the highest commercial standards.
This book has been carefully designed to minimise awkward page turns and
to make playing from it a real pleasure.
Particular care has been given to specifying acid-free, neutral-sized paper made from
pulps which have not been elemental chlorine bleached.
This pulp is from farmed sustainable forests and was produced with special regard for the environment.
Throughout, the printing and binding have been planned to ensure a sturdy,
attractive publication which should give years of enjoyment.
If your copy fails to meet our high standards, please inform us and we will gladly replace it.

**www.musicsales.com**

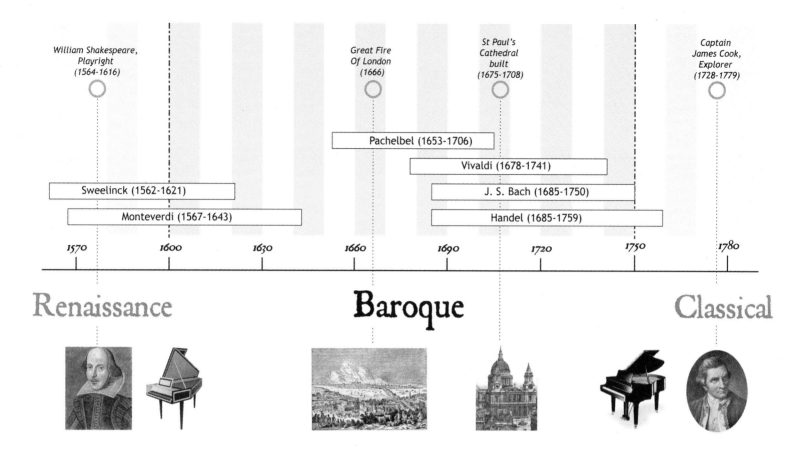

William Shakespeare,
Playright
(1564-1616)

Great Fire
Of London
(1666)

St Paul's
Cathedral
built
(1675-1708)

Captain
James Cook,
Explorer
(1728-1779)

Pachelbel (1653-1706)

Vivaldi (1678-1741)

Sweelinck (1562-1621)

J. S. Bach (1685-1750)

Monteverdi (1567-1643)

Handel (1685-1759)

1570    1600    1630    1660    1690    1720    1750    1780

# Renaissance

# Baroque

# Classical

In music, the term 'Baroque' describes a style of composition reflecting many of the characteristics of the Baroque visual arts including a love of elaborate ornamentation and dramatic contrast. The word Baroque (from the Portuguese word 'barroco' meaning an irregularly shaped pearl) was originally used as a derogatory term to describe music that was excessively complicated and inelegant. The term was not used without its negative connotations until the 20th century.

Baroque music spans a period from c.1600 to c.1750, and found its finest moment in the works of Handel and Bach. It had started as a reaction against the sober rationality of the Renaissance, and resulted in a new enthusiasm among composers keen to explore contrasts in dynamics, tempo, texture, and even architectural space (the Venetian composer Giovanni Gabrieli, for example, composed music where separate choirs sing to one another from different parts of a church building).

Instrumental music became increasingly important in the Baroque period. Previously, most music had been written for voices, and if instruments were used, they would simply play along with vocal parts. The concerto flourished: an instrumental form that delighted in exploring the relationship between soloist and orchestra. Vivaldi's *The Four Seasons* (see p22) is a set of four violin concertos that evoke climatic contrasts found throughout the year but also gives instrumental performers an opportunity to demonstrate their virtuosity.

Opera was also born in the Baroque period. Early operas by Jacopo Peri had been confined to court performances, but not long after Claudio Monteverdi's *Orfeo* had its first performance in 1607, seasons of public operas became established in Italy and the new genre combined solo and choral singing, declamation, acting and dancing.

Another defining characteristic of the Baroque period was the new prominence the bass line received. It became fundamentally important and composers began to use bass lines to create structures. 'Ground bass,' where a repeated bass line underpins the whole composition, is one such device (see Pachelbel's *Canon*, p8 and *When I Am Laid In Earth*, p27).

The period predated the invention of the piano, which blossomed in the Classical era (1750-1810). The keyboard instruments used at the time were the harpsichord (where the strings are plucked rather than struck by hammers) and the organ. Contemporary string instruments in use were the viol family (treble, tenor and bass), the violin family (violin, viola, cello and double bass) and the lute (a guitar-like instrument). Flute, oboe, bassoon and recorder were the main woodwind instruments, and the brass family comprised trumpet, sackbut, trombone and horn.

The pinnacle of Baroque music came in the first half of the 18th century and is best exemplified by the works of two contemporaries: Georg Frideric Handel and Johann Sebastian Bach. Handel was a cosmopolitan figure who finally settled in London, writing the greatest operas of the age, inventing the English oratorio and producing many concertos and concert works. In contrast, Bach spent much of his life in Leipzig where his mastery of part-writing combined with his sublime sense of harmony embraced all the defining characteristics of the Baroque to make him possibly the greatest composer in history.

The next generation (most notably Carl Philipp Emmanuel Bach, Johann Sebastian's son) began to reject the complexity of the high-baroque era, and forged a simpler, more direct style. This led to the birth of classicism, but that is another story. Baroque music stands as a rich and glorious period of music, and in the following pages you will find some of its very finest examples.

# Trumpet Tune

Henry Purcell
(1659-1695)

# Rondino

Jean-Philippe Rameau
(1683-1764)

**Moderato**

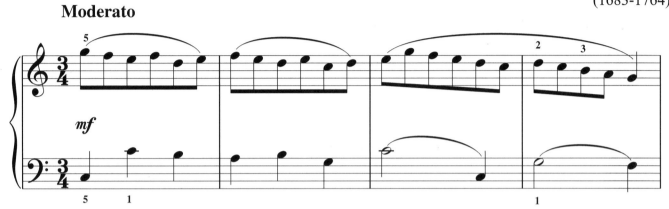

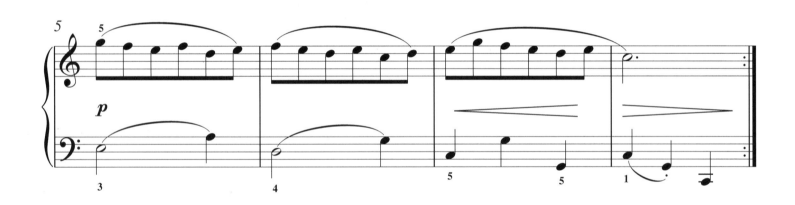

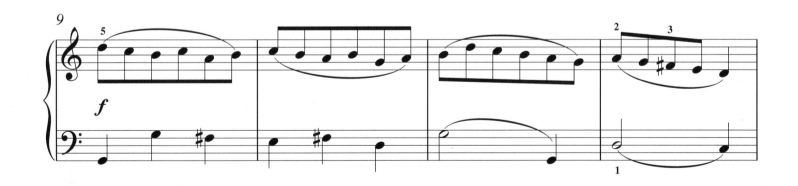

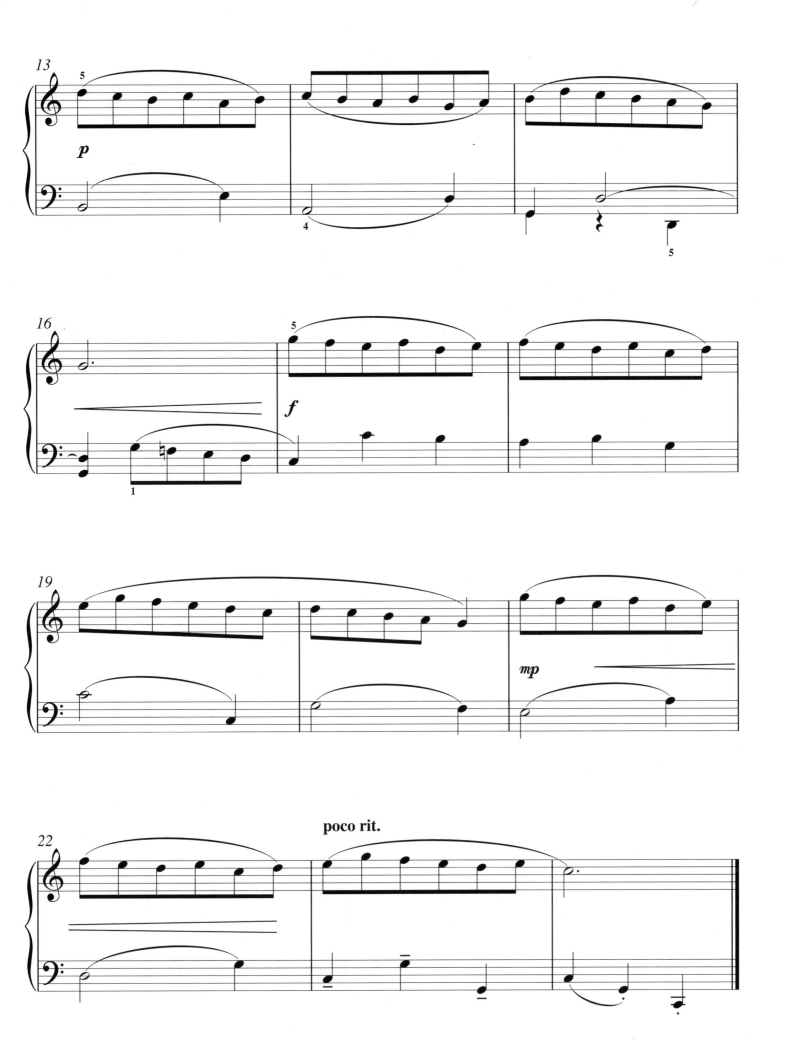

# Canon In D

Johann Pachelbel
(1653-1706)

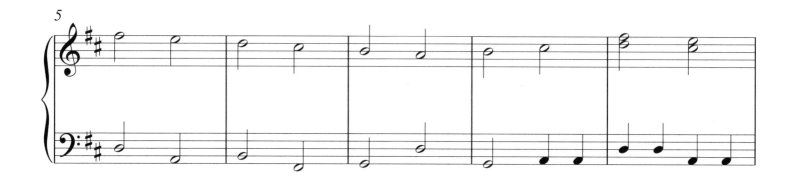

# King William's March

Jeremiah Clarke
(1659-1707)

**Tempo di marche**

# Pavana

Jan Pieterszoon Sweelinck
(1562-1621)

# Largo

Archangelo Corelli
(1675-1726)

# Little Prelude

Domenico Zipoli
(1675-1726)

**Allegro moderato**

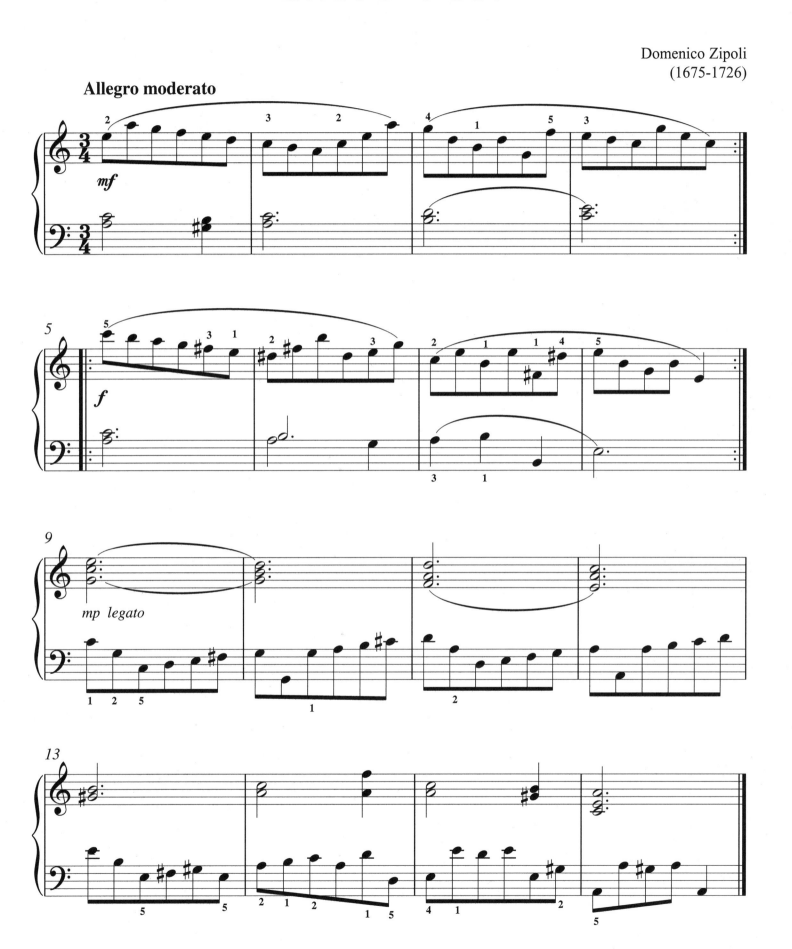

# Little Fugue

Domenico Zipoli
(1675-1726)

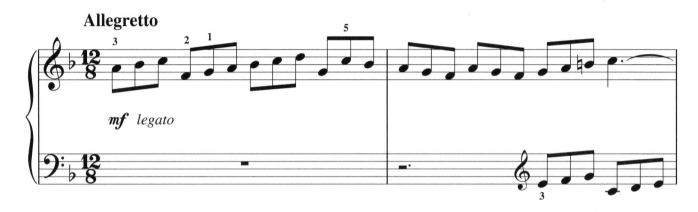

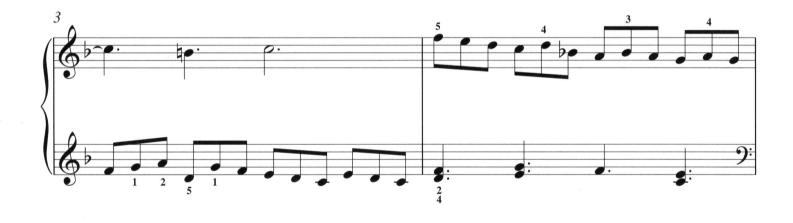

rit.

# Air On The G String

Johann Sebastian Bach
(1685-1750)

# Minuet

Georg Philippe Telemann
(1681-1767)

**Allegretto**

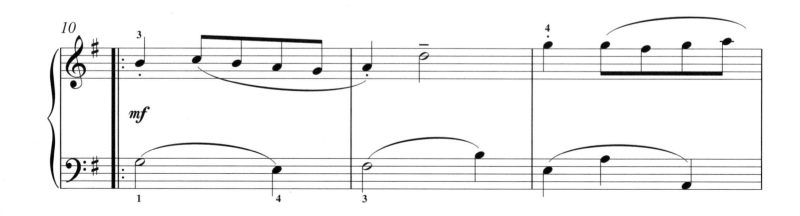

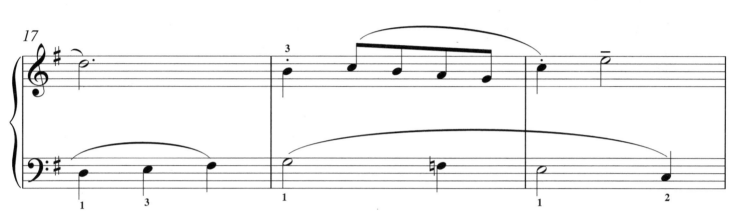

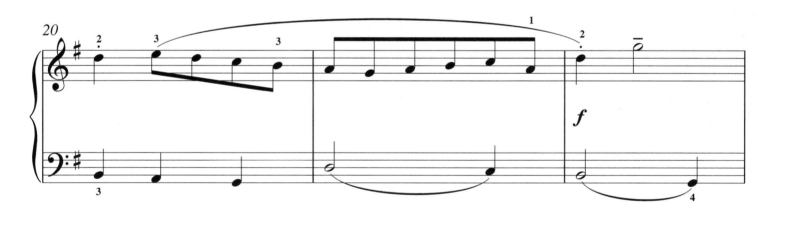

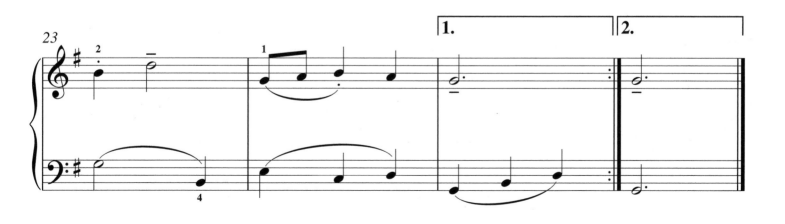

# Adagio Con Espressione

*Sarabande*

Johann Jacob de Neufville
(1684-1712)

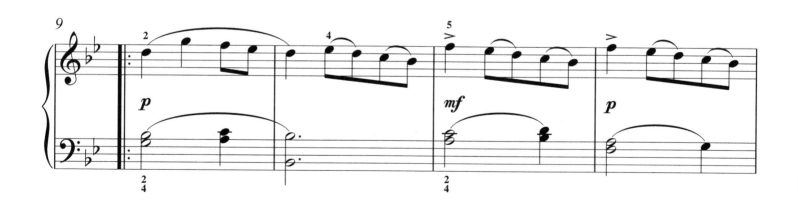

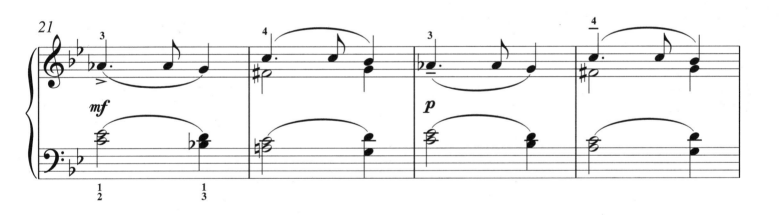

# Autumn (Third Movement)

*from 'The Four Seasons'*

Antonio Vivaldi
(1678-1741)

# Larghetto

Domenico Scarlatti
(1685-1757)

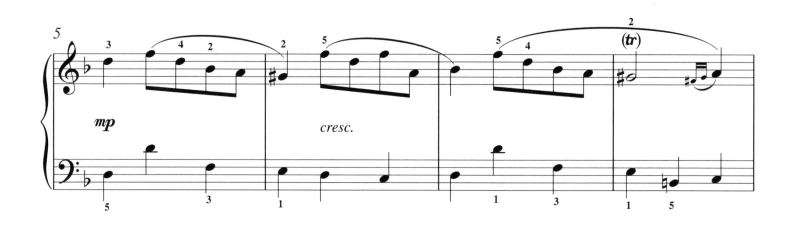

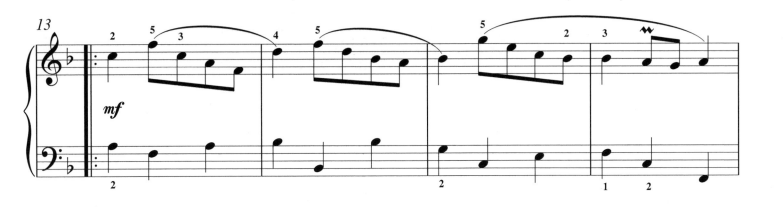

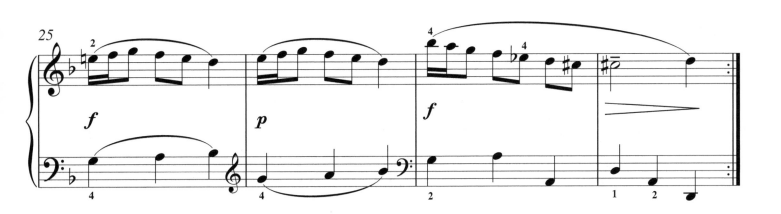

# Little Prelude In C

Johann Sebastian Bach
(1685-1750)

**Allegro moderato**

# When I Am Laid In Earth

*from 'Dido And Aeneas'*

Henry Purcell
(1659-1695)

# Hornpipe

*from 'Water Music'*

Georg Frideric Handel
(1685-1757)

123456789